The Peacock's Cry

edited
by

Karuna Sivasailam

The Peacock's Cry

Published by:
Unisun Publications
Unisun Technologies (P) Ltd,
#7, Floor-1, Kodava Samaja Building
First Main Road, Vasanthnagar, Bangalore 560052, India.
Phone: 91-80-22289290 Fax: 91-80-22289294.
e-mail: info@unisun4writers.com
website: www.unisun4writers.com

First print: February 2006

Typeset and printed by Adprints and Publishers
Mysore Road, Bangalore, India.

Special Indian Price: Rs 125/- only

ISBN 81-88234-23-0

Unisun dedicates this book of poetry

to all Indians & Indophiles

whose hearts beat
for India.

Contents

Foreword

Luckily for us, poetry is not an anachronism, and is well and truly alive despite the SMS lingo that has taken the world by storm. Poetry is a living tradition, and the poetic sensibility is throbbing and thriving. Human emotion, in its purest form – be it love, anger, frustration or sorrow, when truly expressed is always poetic.

Writing poetry in English is not a new phenomenon in India – and now, for most urban Indians, English has become the main language of communication, and some of their most deeply felt emotions and thoughts are expressed in English. And the best part is that modern Indian English poetry is totally in sync with the times.

The Peacock's Cry is about India, and about all those million things that evoke India for us – roadside Ganesha shrines, the cawing of the crows, politicians, torrential monsoons, cricket, kohl-lined eyes, stench of rotting garbage, pine-scented hills, religion – and much, much more. True, this country with its land, ethos, culture, languages, and most importantly its people, is not an experience that can be distilled and expressed in all its totality in a short anthology. Nevertheless the muse of *The Peacock's Cry* is India. All the twelve poets featured in this anthology have captured in their poems that elusive 'Indianness' in some way or the other.

The outer or the visible India – its geography and its landscape, is naturally a major leitmotif. While **Sudipta Chatterjee** talks eloquently about the '…laid-back dunes of golden sand', and the tumbling mountain rivers, **Nikhilesh Dholakia** sings paeans to the burgeoning cityscape and its people.

The inner landscape, the soul of India, is something that all of us Indians carry within us, no matter where we go – which is why we have the Tyagaraja Aradhana in Cleveland and Dandia

Nights in Southall, London. This inner landscape is explored, celebrated and exposed by **Jaya Madhavan** with great sensitivity.

Education, a major concern and obsession of the great Indian middle-class, is a recurring topic, handled by four of our poets in dramatically different ways. While **Biswarup Sarangi** laughingly recalls teenage rebellion and its effective quelling, **Dominic Franks** laments the inevitable loss of innocence, **Lalitha Subramaniam** broods about the pressures of the system on the child and **Eugene D'Vaz** mourns the double standards of the teacher and the preacher.

India's multiple faiths, the beauty of our ancient myths, our obsession with our past, and the number of rituals and traditions that dominate our lives are woven into the psyche of every Indian as **Bhuvana Sankaranarayanan** and **Deepa A** reveal. The deep faith of the mother praying for her errant son, the plight of the widow, the hypocrisy of the pastor, or the desperation of those trying to belong to an alien land, are not new to us, but at every encounter, they do touch a chord deep down. **Srividya** and **Swetha Prakash** effectively bring out the pity and the horror of social evils like child-marriage and bride burning.

Child abuse (another major concern) in a joint family set-up has been movingly portrayed by **Vyjayanthi Subramaniyan**.

An interesting feature of this anthology is the language, which freely incorporates words from Indian languages like Tamil and Bengali. They have been retained (without italics) because that is precisely how most urban Indians speak now. We shift effortlessly from one language to another both in thought and in speech. It is but right that our writing should reflect this.

The beautiful cover and illustrations in this anthology (all in the Warli Folk Art Style) are the creations of one of our poets, Swetha Prakash.

Finally, why the title *The Peacock's Cry*? The peacock, our national bird is an apt icon for the reality that is India. Beautiful and brilliant plumes catch the eye. But its cry is raucous and harsh, yet vibrantly alive – capable of enthralling and shocking us at the same time.

Karuna Sivasailam

Warli Folk Art Style

The illustrations in this book are in the Warli folk art style. The Warli painting is the ritualistic art of the Warli tribe living in Maharashtra. The Warli people embellish their walls with white to invoke their Gods. Typically these paintings show a multitude of tiny human forms, hunting, dancing or cultivating the land. People, animals and trees are captured in daily scenes with elegant lines. The Warli paintings are remarkable as they deftly capture the day-to-day life of the tribal with simple geometric shapes

Jaya Madhavan

Poet and children's novelist, Jaya Madhavan began her writing career as a copywriter and a columnist. Her first novel for children *Sita and the Forest Bandits* published by the Children's Book Trust won the first prize in Shankar's All India Competition for writers of children's books. Her second book for children on the 13th century weaver-poet Kabir is slated for release later this year. Her poem 'Fenugreek' has been chosen for publication in the South Asian Literary Association Journal.

Post Graduate from Jawaharlal Nehru University, New Delhi and M.Phil in English Literature from Chennai University, Jaya uses storytelling, theatre, songs and Carnatic music to create learning modules for children. Jaya has written a number of short stories for children, which have appeared in leading publications. Though she has been writing poetry from the age of fifteen, she prefers her children's writer identity to the poet's. Speaking of her poetry, she says, 'My poems suffer for me, so that I don't. Many are in the nature of swear words I have feared or failed to utter. I have lost count of the number of poems I have written and not bothered to retain.'

Ganesha Speak

From under the tree -
I listen to
the priest chant
the only hymn he knows
just as loud as the clunk of
coin on plate.
Knuckles knocking temples
groans of knees doing sit-ups
dizzy footsteps of the barren
going round around me hissing
chants to go heavy with child,
rustle of arasa leaves and
exploding coconuts.
From under the tree -
I oil the spokes of the
Cosmos
Clog black holes
Sift with sieve
good and bad
from time dunes.

From under the tree -
I survey
street corners for accidents,
subside exam fevers,
remove snags in vahanams… I mean
vehicles,
hunt for the lost diamond earring hidden
beneath the cot
to earn my coconut for the day….
At dusk,
after a hard day's work
I stretch my tusk
when nobody's watching.

A Recipe

To
make a
boneless dough
is not
tough.

The
batter
can be
pulled this way and that,
by hair,
pounded
on nose,
mouth, eye.

That's no matter.

Grab the un-plying whore
by the hull
and on
the wall or door
whichever is
closest, hardest,
smash the skull.

Finally
when of desirable consistency
leave behind
closed door
for the unbaked to rise
(rant or heave)
while you rest your fist.

Much later
raise the lid
to see if
dough is set.
If still loose,
it can be
made to coagulate
on its own
or with some help.

But what
may not gel
for your immediate requirements
are the
bleeding
memories.

Migratory Birds

Two crows scout in roguish weather
flown from India
without feathers or coat
to nestle in.

All white breaks loose
as we bury
ancestor's
well maintained purity,
who never
leapt across seas,
ate meat or wine.

Here amidst stubborn pines
who keep on their green all year round
the crows dart.

'I am Ravi Mathur. I am here 25 years.
Visited India 8 times hence. This my wife Carolyn.'
Unruly Indian tongue
well kneaded into
smoothest dough
for banana bread.

He rolls -
slurring and slurping,
eager to put mouth on alien breast.
I turn,
sick in stomach.

In a land of
seagulls
the crows
try to merge with snow.

Sepia

On two sides of that one street
Are two houses
Built, rebuilt and expanded
In my one dream too often dreamt.

Pinkish, rigid, mutely lighted
Owned by a hag who drives a beetle
With spiked whip and heavy pounds
Gathered in mind, soul and dripping chin.

I dripped my first flush of brown there
In an otherwise
Primary world.
The cackle of that witch's joy
Matched my fear.

So your uyir * departs this way
Like iodine tears shed
Over brown paper covers
Hastily torn off rusting notebooks
To hide the bleeding shame of
Premature death.

Tepid coffee for the dying while
Fingers bloom mehendi flowers.
Amma wraps my first sari
'But where is your hip, my girl?'

The fusty cobweb.
The happy sparrows.
Peeping brothers and

Whispering elders
All wait.

I await the witch.
No one is telling me,
Why I must dribble in public?
Why my piddle now is so precious
And bronzed?

She comes.
The pride of owning two pinkish houses
On that one street
Oozing through her stained teeth.

'Chocolates, brownies, tasty tans,
Now belong to Peter Pan.
I shall now do what I can
To find the right sized Superman.'

Sprinkling and spitting,
The baptism grows.
'Icy hymen, waiting semen.
But when in heat go mate a woman.'

A picture hangs by the window
Framing me with her
White flowers in hair
Black tremors in heart
I stand.
Rigid.
Newly armed with knowledge
On how to battle tainting curses with pads in purses.
Or how to hide the sultry tree growing between my legs.

Walled in, strung high and bleeding between teeth
The rotting picture still instructs,
'When in heat go mate a woman.'
The tree rustles too tightly for comfort.
Writhing in heat,
The burning bromide now smiles,
Her brown,
Very warm, very knowing sepia.

uyir: Tamil word meaning life

From an Office Window

Have you watched a crow
polish off a rat?
I did.
Yesterday.

Well,
the juicy entrails long
winding and twisted
into gossip, go first.

The rat's innards flow.
First fluently.
Then
h a l t i n g l y
in small talk.

Coming to the heart of the matter.
The nervy crow
picks up an arterial thread
from a crisscross
of thoughts and treads across
meatydetailssilentspacesfatunshedandsuddenly

                              p
                            u

                    s
                  k
                r
              e
            j

to nibble on a memory.

Elsewhere
two clock hands
come together
in a beak, closing
to devour time,
memories,
conversations.

Then comes the kidney.
But much water has already flown.
What use is a dead rat?
Or so I thought.

The glutton picks the bones clean.
Slowly, surely, leisurely.
Every peck, a jab at time.

The crow relishes the memory
of the rat that once was,
and I remember our
old conversations.

At the Laundromat

In my country
Gods pace restlessly
waiting to be born.
Waiting for injustice
to compel them
to incarnate.

We also
celebrate
every month
without fail
three days of
red untouchability.

Girls shall protect their
virginity for their fathers'
mapillais'- who are no less
than Maha Vishnu.
Marry to
beget sons for the dynasty,
commit not the blasphemy of
talking back to
errant husbands.

Earth revolves,
Sun shines,
Stars stand,
Gravity stays,
Rains fall,
because of us
chaste
women.

Draw water from a well.
When husband calls
Just drop the rope and run.
The water filled bucket
shall wait stand still
halfway up the well
till you come back to draw it.
(Ah! But only if you are
the best of wives.)
And such sophisticated chastity tests
we have.

Amidst dirty linen
washed in public
I
much married,
heavily untouchable,
with public as witness,
explore a sexy neckline.
Trifle prickly,
but deliciously alien.

The machines foam
and froth at the mouth.
Do they already know?
Snow White dripping red
has carelessly affected
the geopolitics of her country.

* *mapillai: Tamil word for groom*

Dowhrudhini*

Mud
Fresh and damp
Ash
Grey and warm
Mango
Sour, very sour.

I need
for my heart
to descend from
chest
to rest
in a belly of water
billowing,
brimming,
beating.

Touching parts of the earth
I sense -
tremors of clay shaping,
tidal lashing
of my heart
nurturing its voice
standing neck deep in water.

Nine months, nine days,
the wheel turns
while I potter about
with dreams,
labouring
on small feats
in between
throwing up,
bites of life.

Then comes a sound,
first tiny,
then thunderous.
Seeking its own heart,
separate mind, soul,
for its body no longer wet.
Quake
    after quake
        after
           quake
of divorce
ascends my heart
forcibly
back to the cage of ribs.
Between lightnings of pain
Claps of tumult and mutiny
I
now of one heart,
kneel,
to deliver the voice,
kicking and crying
at the mouth
of birth
to be thrown on the wheel of life.

If My Son Were a painter

I'd let him paint me
in the nude.
Breasts, buttocks, scars
Caesarean
and everything
underneath.

Don't you own my body
in sly
clammy hugs,
or make yourself
masseur
to caress anointments on
aching
false bottoms.

See me in full,
not as a bath aftermath
or your father's favourite
piece of ass.
But as a woman, a mother, a bitch,
furniture
if need be.

Look at me
straight in the eye,
when you sketch your
sketches of love.
Brush as you wish.
Hard strokes, soft strokes,
do them all.

Please your palette.
Then grab Oedipus
by the horn
and show him the door.

My son.
My nudity is not my shame.
Nor yours.
My nudity.
Your freedom.

Now go,
Love, own,
give
a woman completely.
Be MY son.

Purposely Politically Incorrect

Janardhana!
More than anything
what I want to do is,
pull you out of your
serpentine water bed
and repair to the beach
with you
aerially.

Take a mango frond from the
beachside stall
and comb your hair
till it smells of
sticky sour milk.
Find few seashells,
shake sand off to
make a string of
sounds
with conches.
Seat you in the beach
sand in sand
Janardhana
seat you sand in sand,
holding hand in hand,
just so you don't run
while I tell you
how you broke
(not heart, not mind)
how you broke
a lump of lung
of windy consistency.
Now does that ring a chime?

Janardhana,
while you grow lotuses
out of your navel
just so they can shoot and bend
to keep your nostrils fragrant,
while you enjoy
the pressing work
at your feet
a
damsel delivers....

Think Janardhana
of what remains between us,
what you owe me
and also of your swanky mid ocean resort.
My Lord,
I am no Goddess
to undress at your will
before you and your stupid snake -
six heads in all
for nought.
It is not just you
who can make
one's world fall in
like telescoping spine.
I can make you remain here forever
sticky hair, loud garland and all
counting the grains of sand on the beach
waiting for me to fetch food for you after office.

If you don't watch it
Janardhana,
right in front of your

one thousand eyes
I shall pee to curdle
your ocean of milk
to make your lady get up
bleary eyed
sneeze a piddly sneeze and glide away
in her night clothes,
your slithery bed scrambling after her.

Biswarup Sarangi

Biswarup Sarangi originally hails from the Steel City of Jamshedpur, Jharkhand.

An architect by profession, he now lives and works in Bangalore. Besides writing poetry, he also dabbles in prose and painting (in various media) and has had several exhibitions of his paintings. He started writing a few years ago; as a quicker means of gratification when the palette ran dry. A few of his poems have been published in local journals.

8190 Down Alleppey Tata

The train stops yet again,
It is one of those stations in Andhra,
That almost as a norm,
Has more letters in its name,
Than people on the platform,
Thalepaligudem.

A strapping, lithe woman stands ready,
With a basket of guavas held aloft,
Picked off the nearby trees,
That hang over the corrugated roof.
The canteen vendor sits near the bridge,
Fanning formidable Bhajjis in his stall,
The kind that's certain to keep the tongue ablaze,
Through Orissa till West Bengal.

Further down, huddled on a bench,
Sits an unsure, lost family of four,
Dressed in bright clothes, waiting
For the start of their rare one day tour.

Outside his room, the stationmaster stands,
Waving the green flag at the guard,
The train eases out of Thalepaligudem,
After its quiet and brief sojourn.

Awe

My father would fret and flare:
'The colour tube will lose its life!'
I was around ten,
And would stay glued to the TV for hours,
(It being a novelty then)
I used to imagine
Colour being squeezed
Onto the screen from behind,
Much like toothpaste from a tube.

Bioscopewala

At the cross roads he'd come and stand,
With his box and brass bell in hand,
His apparatus -
Three oil tins nailed, painted bright,
Slung over the shoulder at waist height,
And for eight annas he would unfurl,
The realms of a magical world;
Every time that he would come,
He'd have a newly woven tale with him,
Myths, history, events and places,
Would roll past the rapt faces,
Huddled and clashing around the peephole,
To be the first one to be shown.

And then -
With the advent of the centrepiece,
Of urban life in the late eighties,
His voice lost its allure,
Slowly became rare,
While the young stayed indoors,
Spellbound and in thrall,
Of the relentless magic machine,
That rang his death knell and did him in.

Many summers later,
The word of his demise got through,
From our new maid,
In a tone of detached woe,
And also the news
That he was buried not very far,
From the newly erected TV tower

End Game

In the last few months at school
The boys would stay back late to try,
And connive new pranks
To play on their tormentors,
To forever remember them by.
On one such Saturday-
After many stunts were mooted and rejected,
Somebody from the back half-heartedly said,
'How about if we all just go
And shave all our f'king heads?'
There was an immediate furore of approval.
At the battle cry uttered -
Not a moment too soon,
Off we marched in unison,
To the nearest propitious saloon.
Monday morning at assembly,
We stood out like a pack of sore thumbs,
But despite the wholly overt outrage,
We thought we carried it off with aplomb.
Later that day-
The rule books were poked and trashed in vain,
By the vexed teachers till very late,
To throw a pertinent law with relish,

At our contemptuous bald pates.
When they finally blew the bugle,
We knew they'd pondered really hard,
For their wily chastisement,
Caught the entire tenth standard off guard.

The Principal came to our class and announced:
'Socials will be held this week!'
The annual charade with our counterparts,
At the Sacred Heart Convent - across the street;
Those girls after our torturous hearts!
This rather cunning retort,
Threw the delinquents into panic,
And sent us scurrying for desperate measures
Like wigs, shady hats and hair growth tonics.
After much grim deliberation,
It was finally decreed,
To face death with dignity,
But to lessen the deed,
By walking in unselfconsciously,
- Hale and hearty,
With the pretext of a costume party.
On 'Socials' night
Everybody turned up in drag,
(As the 'Coneheads' clan.)
But the story was out -
And our cover up sagged;
The long cherished night
Was reduced to one of shame,
As we were left listening to sniggers,
Beaten at our very own game.
For some time -
Our sorry farce put to rest,

The piquant ritual,
Of passers out playing the jest,
Or ready to break any Godforsaken rule,
At Jamshedpur Loyola High School.
But can nifty minds be kept down for long?
This year the tenth standard was again on song,
On their last day the boys turned up in shorts,
Back to basics gear -
Water bottle, ID card and lunch box,
And made their feelings sweetly apparent,
When they went and sat in kindergarten.

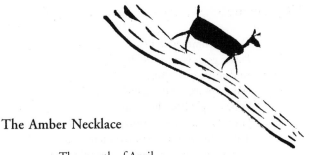

The Amber Necklace

The month of April-
The dry and dense woods
On the mountain range
Cradling the city,
Would burst into flames,
And spread till
The vagrant flares had burnt
An irregular pulsating line
On the crown of the invisible hill.
It'd send the recently retired
Wild elephants, deer and foxes,
Scurrying for shelter down the slope,
From its barrage of blinding heat,
Snapping of wood, falling branches and smoke;
The wildfire would sprout offshoots,
Start to ebb out,
Break away,
Like huge rubies strung on thin cotton,
Spring back to life,
Dance with the winds,
Till around ten;
And not leave a trace of its fury
For next morning,
Come evening, it'd start again.

This Country

On hot summer nights,
Power grids would run dry
And entire townships
Would plunge into darkness;
Folks would be reduced to
Groping and sweating around Petromax lamps,
Till the lights were restored at ten,
Not out of any apparent consideration
For the suffering populace,
But to prevent the expensive high tension wires
From being cut and stolen.

Dance of Death

They arrived on jittery bicycles
Chased by a gang of ragged boys,
With their pillion passengers
Perilously poised,
Then announced the show
With practiced pomp and flair,
Sending shivers of excitement
Through the idle morning air,
Pulling in the vile throngs
And wagers from their hands,
As the handsome pair
Was placed on its last stand,
For folks to weigh their chances
And place their stakes,
On the swifter wielder
Of a four inch blade;
The yet innocent fairground
Acquired a ghastly twist,
As the shadows grew shorter,
And the baying reached a high pitch,
The doomed pair was ceremoniously blessed
And finally let loose,
A rapture of sunflowers at their necks,
A flurry of steel at their toes,
The bilious rabble fell over
In trepidation for their placed bets,
As the cocks circled each other,
And did the dance of death.

Like a Gentleman

True to the word
Whether we got a chance to pad up at all,
Or were left to languish
Near the kits,
Shadow-batting our sore wrists
Till noon,
We would turn up for nets
Every winter morning,
With freshly whitened keds
White flannels and V-necked sweaters,
The India emblem woven
To various degrees of accuracy,
Ready to impress
Upon the coach,
The courage behind
Five kilos worth of padding,
And an abdominal guard
One size too big.

Vastu Utsav

They dug up the tome
And placed it on our chests,
Read it backwards to dictate
The terms for our supposed
Interest,
Where we're bound to do
Not what'd suit us fine,
But as prescribed
By the speckled letters
Divine,
Leaving us in charge
Of issues as grave,
As deciding bathroom tile colours,
And patterns for door
Architraves.

This Country II

The same people who reverentially wriggle up
From their hard fought seats on buses
To stand for a full fifteen minutes,
When going over the holy Ganges,
Can be found lolling around
On bouncy rexine sofas at home,
In an effort to stretch forever
Those elusive red-letter commemoratives
In August or January,
When the national anthem
Is played early morning on TV.

From a Distance

The passage of fleeting trains
Whistling over the penta-arched bridge,
And through the dense foliage,
Far beyond our three-storied ancestral house
As the sun finally heaved and sank for the day
Into its pillow of clouds,
Would have us drawn on our tip toes
To the crusty parapet on the roof;
The carefully monitored progress
Of the evening on the Ludo board
Abandoned in our excitement.

Decades later…
On my way home once a year,
When I think we're close to the same village,
I dodge a dozen people
To get to the door on the train
For a hopeful glimpse in the clear,
Of the staid bearer of the family's fortunes,
Now devoid and locked,
As generations have scattered
Like glistening marbles from tiny hands..
I must admit
I'm yet to spot the building.

The Cursed Well

My head spins
And I force a grimace,
To get my eyes back into focus
Onto the kids getting wheeled
Deliriously in shopping carts,
As they lean out and grab
At the vacuum-sealed poly packs,
Off the high shelves
In this sanitized high temple
Of swipe-card redemption;
I look around in forced reverence,
And I listen-
Not to the inane music on the local FM,
Or the contented blabber of the fortunate few
At the altar-
In a righteous queue,
But to the argument between
The walls of my stomach
And the empty space within.

Musk

After a mile long hike
I boarded a bus,
But gave up my seat
Feeling rather magnanimous,
To a blind man
Who came and stood
Too close to me
To ignore for good
The sublime joy I felt
Though soon gave way,
To hurt, shock and then dismay,
When my beneficiary yielded his place,
To some chappan churi*
Wrapped in a skirt, ribbons and lace.

*chappan churi: Hindi slang for a sharp and dangerous woman;
like fifty six knives

Home

A few snatches of lost tunes
Sometimes float over these dunes
And tug at the heart,
The land we left
Across seven seas
Estranged, bereft.
Every once in a while
We promise ourselves
A journey home
This year or next
Then lose resolve
When we finally know
Nobody sings those songs
Anywhere, anymore.

Cheese

I wheel my bags
Packed with six months supply
Of essential spices
An assortment of itchy new knitwear,
And all my precious prejudices
Towards the draped conveyor belt,
No emotional baggage,
No umbilical guilt;
While I wait
The mounted TVs talk glib,
About inner boundaries
That discomfortingly fracture,
Even as more exacting outer ones
Soften up conspicuously and blur;
So before the final battle lines are drawn,
I need to get counted in
Come what may,
I'll take my chances and hitch on;
Hullo- brave new world!
I'm on my way.

The Pounding

I stumbled on
With stoic shoes,
The years they
Took their toll,
Till one fine day
My toes hit dirt,
And I landed
At the mender of soles';
Said I -
'I've trudged
For twenty years
And still
I'm caught between
The hammer and the
Confounded anvil
I'm bent, I'm sore,
And I now I find,
Myself in line for
Another thirty years
Of the grind!'
He chuckled as I ranted
And moved so niftily,
He almost sewed
His nimble fingers
Up with my battered shoes,
Then handed them back
From under his blue umbrella,
And said, 'Son,
Haven't you learnt
About the Law
Of diminishing returns?

Whores in White

Five years of filth
Have washed us by,
And on our porch
Stand the whores in white;
With starched suits,
Clasped hands
And utter shamelessness,
They march to the trough-
The marketplace;
They mount a podium,
Then plead and beg,
The privileged ones-
To repeat their mistakes;
The entourage announces plans
And elucidates work done,
Amidst the gathered
Curious and jaded ones;
They cringe not at the stink
Or the unholy sights,
They're good at it
These whores in white.
Banners are hoisted
And leaflets brought out,
To pass amidst the now
Coiled evening crowd,
Someone then passes
A gleeful word
down the rank,
'The bridge is down
We've taken out the planks!'
The placebos they mouth
Won't save their lives
This time we'll get
The whores in white.

Deepa A

Deepa A is a journalist currently based in New Delhi. She began her career with *The Indian Express* in Mumbai and has since worked with *The Times of India* in Mumbai and Hyderabad. She has a keen interest in reporting development-related issues, and has written many articles on education, health and environment for various Indian publications. She also writes poetry and short stories and has an abiding passion for books, movies and music — strictly in that order. Her works have appeared in *The Little Magazine* and *Outlook Traveller*.

A Year Later

On the wall
above his writing desk,
a row of gods
watch him scribble
letters to the editor,
about kings without kingdoms
and maids who were once queens.
Under the banyan tree
the stone snake,
we appease with milk
every evening,
the ground a swirl of brown leaves
rustling under our feet
as we try to be quietly pious.
In his doctor's handwriting
that none of us can decipher,
he wonders about the family curse,
the sword that no longer hangs
in the living room,
the gravestones in the backyard,
the pain of outliving daughters
and granddaughters.
I learn all this
from the astrologer
who smiles at me after lunch.
He is here
to find from stars and planets
why there's no laughter in our house.
In alignments that we cannot see,
he finds the veins of a curse
throbbing with our tears.

The snake god has to be moved,
he says gravely,
to the garden with
gooseberries and jasmines.
Perhaps we made too much noise
when we lit lamps at dusk.
She always laughed the loudest.
On the day she died,
she woke up smiling
remembering my fear
of yakshis,* the white hands I saw
stretching from the shivering leaves
of the banyan tree
calling us home.

yakshi: female spirit, often considered an enchantress

The River Has Its Reasons

The master carpenter
dropped an axe
on his son's neck,
out of envy perhaps
or loathing
even the legends are uncertain.
Behind the temple
the river
flows silently,
unhurriedly .
Here on the steps
leading to the god carved in stone,
the story of the son
who predicted
the river would flow this way
one day.
His father
embarrassed
by this knowledge
and maybe a little jealous
praying to the river
asking her to deviate from a path
she has already chosen.
This temple
past paddy fields and banyan trees
with its flagstaff and metal bells
held together by faith
the symbol of an answered prayer.

Yet, every monsoon
a billowing river

reaches up to the steps,
drowning the god
we appease with garlands
and sandalwood paste
on other days.
Swirling in her muddy waters
wobbly lines of remorse,
I know this to be her apology
to the son long dead.

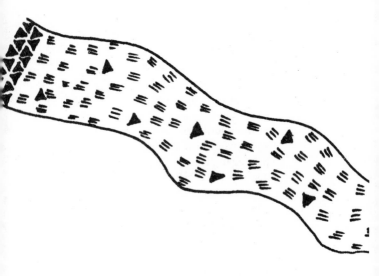

Lalitha Subramaniam

A postgraduate in English literature with some teaching experience, she has been writing since over a decade but not published anything substantial. Her main interests are reading, writing, cinema and music. Her reading eclectic, mainly non fiction and some amount of fiction, her favourite authors being PG Wodehouse, Richard Gordon, Sue Townsend, John Grisham, Paul Theroux and Vikram Seth.

She believes that she has been particularly influenced by Emily Dickinson's terse epigrammatic style. Besides poetry, she does book and film reviews. A few of her poems were published on *Sulekha* website.

The Race

The race began
bright one morn,
at age three and one quarter.
His dress was blue,
mood too,
as he wailed a 'Ta-Ta' to her.
Eat your biscuit.
Write that 'A'.
Mama'll come, never fear.
Thus they piled
the unwilling child,
with numbers, rhymes,
big words too.
The hour went by,
Mama came.
He learned to wipe his tears,
to bend with weight
of bag and breathe
a mix of chalk, chemistry and Shakespeare.
The years sped past,
and soon he was peering
and searching for his blessed Roll number.
'Aha! I've made it....
But just about,
with a percentage of 95.8.
He strolled through college.
Read, sang, danced.
These surely were wonderful years!
Degree in hand,
he cried, 'I'm first!'
Poor sod.
He knew not,
the next lap had just begun.

A Teacher's Plaint

A gaggle of eager young faces
Waiting to be spoon-fed and taught,
Each morn all eyes look up hopeful-
'Will today's lesson be short?'
A group of somnolent students
Doze thru' the post-lunch first hour.
'Any questions, doubts; shall I proceed?'
The silence is severed by a snore.
A bunch of hyperactive pre-teens
Await the day's final bell.
Books are hunted, bags shut -
Clang rush, ouch!
Teacher fell.

Nikhilesh Dholakia

Nikhilesh Dholakia writes poetry and fiction from cross-cultural and global perspectives. His creative writing interests date back to childhood days when he and a fellow student produced a handwritten magazine for the private reading pleasure of family and friends. Some writing continued in college days in the 1970s, and then tapered off – only to be rekindled by visits to the fast-changing India of the 2000s.

When not doing creative writing, Nikhilesh can be found lecturing in the classrooms of the College of Business Administration at the University of Rhode Island (URI) in USA. Nikhilesh and his scholar-professor wife Ruby Roy Dholakia have their home on the shores of a cove off the Atlantic Ocean in Rhode Island, the tiniest of the 50 states and one of the original 13 colonies that formed the United States of America.

A Dollar in Kolkata

> George Washington framed
> In silver curled mane
> Waistcoat with silk cravat
> Hint of Mona Lisa smile
> A dollar in the wallet
> 'Forty-five... today's rate'
> Add a few pennies
> Fifty rupees
> Five crumpled notes
> Reddish pink with
> Mahatma's serene eyes

Silicon Valley nemesis
Verdant floral campus of Infosys
Trendy Bangalore techies
Lounging in cafeteria in faded jeans
'We price in dollars,' the CFO beams
'A dollar buys two scoops of ice cream'

> Outskirts of Ahmedabad
> Multiplexes and malls
> Gobbling up farmland
> Every few yards, pizza stalls
> How many rupees... fifty?
> If lucky, a ticket to the matinee

Outlying village, that's what this was
Manoeuvring grey Hyundai amidst subji-wallahs
It's no longer Delhi, we call it NCR
National Capital Region,
Stretching from Noida to Gurgaon

Fifty rupees may still get you
A hamburger and Coke at Nirula's.

    Imposing gothic railway terminus
    No longer Victoria's, that's Shivaji's bust
    This is the heart of Bombay
    From Marine Lines to Backbay
    Fifty rupees, at the old taxicab rate
    May get you from VT to Churchgate

Crisp, chilly December Kolkata air
Major exhibit at Fine Arts Academy
Across in the Maidan, a Fair
Jhaal Muri, multihued bangles
Handloom saris, a merry affair
Rabindra sangeet and Christmas jingles
How cute... Jamini Roy copies
Madam, my own short stories
Struggling writer, Sir; self-published book
I'm art student, Madam; please look
How much are these?
Framed painting? Book of stories?
Very cheap – only fifty rupees!

At the Edge of India

Winding highway through the hills
Snaking lines of lorries
Bearing food and petrol
Crossing paths with trucks
Laden with wood and coal
Commerce of dependence
At the edge of India

Perched on stilts
Neat huts of bamboo lattice
Red mud packed soft hills
Perpetual candidates
For precipitous landslides
Stunning tribal lasses
By huts and hamlets
Not quite Mongol
Not quite Caucasian
Aquiline traces
On Asiatic faces
Creeping Indianization
Rakish chunni
Draped on tribal skirt
Occasional flashy sari
Dangling earrings
Fashionable bindi

Bollywood style
Embellishing
Raw tribal beauty
Jesus mural
With outstretched arms
Looking down bemusedly
At Hindu tinged
Veneer of modernity
Encroaching silently
On simple Naga Christianity.
Secretive separatist militias
Playing hide and seek
With massive Indian forces
Sporadic ambushes
Demands for autonomy
Calls for cultural purity
Occasional torching
Of hapless village cinema
Exhibiting
Racy Bollywood fare
Hip-swinging filmy popularity
Clashing with unsustainable calls
For cultural chastity
At the edge of India.

Military convoys
Wary, watchful jawan
Fingering the trigger
On cab-mounted gun
Amidst the mélange
Of commerce and culture
In the verdant valleys
Of the rising sun

Lorries and lasses
Guns at mountain passes
Belching smoke
Of semi-burnt diesel
The smell of development
Collisions colourful
Of native and hegemonic sentiment
Overloaded speeding trucks
With poorly maintained brakes
Accidents of progress
By crystal blue lakes
Ultra-hip rock bands
Courted by global media
In the abode of the clouds
At the edge of India.

Sweet Terrorists

I spotted them first
In Ho Chi Minh City
Dotting the phalanx of mobikes
Covered from head to toe
In flowing soft white Ao Dai
Slit stylishly high above waist
Feet planted, waiting for Green
Elbow length white gloves
Faces wrapped in Euro-scarves
Donning caps
Goggles piercing the traffic
Saigon sirens
Waiting to outgun
Hapless male riders on either side

Their Ahmedabad cousins
Swathed in a riot of colour
Sometimes jeans, rarely skirts
Most likely in salwaar-kameez
Chunnis wrapped from heads to necks
Colourful masks revealing only specs
Coming from all sides
Zipping on scooters
Usually single, sometimes a pair
Weaving, dodging
People, bikes, cows and cars
What's that, a slung bazooka?
No just a tight-rolled umbrella
Warding pollution, protecting skin-
Scooter-riding Sweet Terrorists.

Jasmine Choice

Semi-crushed bud
Of jasmine, still fragrant
At pillow's edge
Slight mascara smudge
Wistful reminders
Of sensory overload
- * -
Parted vermilion lips
Filigreed henna patterns
From palm to toes
Serpentine braid
Of strung jasmine, dark locks
Tinkling bells
Adorning anklet and wrist
Carelessly tossed aside
Embroidered magenta silk
Crystalline laughter
Like a cool monsoon mist
- * -
Which one shall I choose?
Manageable memory
Tinged with mild, sweet pain
Or
Overpowering reality
That senses can't contain?

Platform Thirteen

Seven in the morning
Bridled bedlam
The daily scene
Howrah Station's
Platform Thirteen
Masses of multihued humanity
Lugging tiffins, trunks, knapsacks
Rushing to or from trains
Jostling the occasional suited sahib
Skirting the rare-mini-skirted babe
Exchanging staccato conversation, occasional hale
Bengali, Bhojpuri, Oriya, Maithili spew over rail
Red-shirted porters
Muscular, gnarled, brash
Darting with long wooden carts
Parting the swirling crowds
With clanging steel pirate hooks
Bulging tight-sewn sacks
From farms of the East, factories North
Merchandise-bearing monsters
Of white and grey cloth
Concealing mysterious myriad contents
Waiting for the porters' pirate hooks
To be gored
And carted

From Platform Thirteen
To urban godowns unseen
People and parcels
Vendors of victuals

Tugging children, frenetic travellers
Thousand near misses
Of passengers and porters
Computerized control rooms
Directing crowbar wielding linesmen
Trilingual digital displays
Blaring loudspeaker announcements
Jabs of modernity
Piercing the grimy murkiness
Of crumbling colonial carpentry
Spilling endlessly out of
Platform Thirteen
Disgorged masses of mofussil humanity
Packed in buses and rickshaws
Or simply on foot
Along with packed products in sacks
Loaded on lorries, pushcarts, proletarian backs
Crossing the swift-moving currents
Of the muddy grey Hoogly
Over the hoary Howrah Bridge
Through the charred wood smog
Towards the shimmering promise
Of the Great Eastern Metropolis.

Beauty of Kolkata

I know…
Beauty is universal
No boundaries, no race.
From summits to oceans
Grace defies place
But in Kolkata
Smoggy, chaotic megalopolis
Femininity breaks all rules
From riverbanks to choked streets
The Bengali Beauty rules
Those mysterious eyes
Barely smiling, possibly inviting
Questioning, judging, reassuring
Sensuously shy
Stridently demanding
Subtly signalling
Romance: possibly explosive, likely enduring
Those mellifluous notes
Wafting down labyrinthine lanes
Celebratory or melancholy
Musical conversations
From the pages of Geetanjali
Bottled passion
Flowing through chords, sitar and vocal
Melodies of Tagore and Nazrul
Mingling with
Classical ragas and chart-topping yodel
Those mesmerizing hues
Of cottons, georgettes and silks

Neither Bollywood brash nor Delhi dash
Just wispy, soothing, languid flows
Of understated elegance
Be it dupattas, sari pallus, or knitted throws
Grace trumps chic, the Bengali Beauty knows
Demure or dramatic
In virulent demon-slaying frenzy
Or in states of tranquil catharsis
In all resplendent forms, feminity converges
In the Great Eastern Metropolis.

Vyjayanthi Subramaniyan

Vyjayanthi Subramaniyan completed M.B.B.S from Bangalore Medical College and M.D in Psychiatry from National Institute of Mental Health And Neurological Sciences [NIMHANS]. She is currently practicing Psychiatry privately. Married to a lawyer and mother of a little boy, Vyjayanthi is settled in Bangalore.

Vyjayanthi was the lead actress in the Kannada film, *Huvu Hannu* and is also the member of the theatre group, Spandana. She has anchored talk shows on television and has had her short stories published in the Kannada magazine, *Sudha*.

Gandhari

She blinded her eyes,
She did not see
Her husband, who
Could not see her.

She never saw the world
Her husband did not see.
So believed the world.

The world could only see
What it wanted to see.

Scratches Over Ink Stains

She was fair, I was dark.
She had short curly hair.
I had long straight hair.
She from central board school,
high standards, unthinkable for a
state school scholar
like me.
She had a sophisticated English accent
to her mother tongue,
while I was tongue-tied.
She even laughed when asleep,
I only managed a smile for the audience.
She danced with delight,
I danced with disease.
She had an older brother
protecting her,
I had an older sister
attacking me.

She cannot sing, only bray
sneered my sister.
She cannot dance, can't even walk
jeered my cousin sister.
Thus they revelled in their
Rivalry.

I did not remain in the shadows,
I was the shadow.
This battlefield was once my mother's nest.
So, I call it Grandpa's house.
In this arena of arrogance,
there was a backyard
which I explored meekly
where plants of jasmine flowers
longed to be watered by me.
An anonymous exotic bird
dropped its colourful feathers,
collector's items for my small box.
My cousin wanted a playmate
who spoke of princes
and princesses with fervour.
My sister demanded non-participation.
I was her possession, obedient slave.

As I sneezed in the attic
over dusty dreamy old classics,
the warm weight of my baby cousin on my lap,
prized possession of my cousin.
Her older brother crept up beside me,
a warm arm surrounded me.
Bewildered, believing the blessing
of a new found elder brother,
a demigod, protector almighty.

He reaffirmed with words
his appreciation of my meekness
gentle suggestion to continue in
gentleness.

He called it femininity.
Confused by actions, snared by words
belying protection,
boasting of brotherly love.
They are virtual viragos,
but you, a venerable virgin,
a lily amongst violets.
 He said he liked me
more than my cousin,
his own sister.
My heart burst with pride.

He caressed me,
but it wasn't
like the feather of an exotic bird.
It wasn't on the exposed skin.
He licked me.
It wasn't like that of my puppy's.
It did not tickle.
Frightened, I cowered
under bed covers.
I crossed my arms across my chest,
an attempt to hide myself.
He leered,
are you holding yourself in check?

I was forced to enter
his room on an errand,
as he poured over best sellers.
So, you could no longer restrain,
with contempt he laughed
at my inarticulate fear,

misinterpreted as coquetry.
If I walked away,
I was playing hard to get he said.
If I walked near, I was mad
with an insatiable drive he said.

Haunted, stifling sobs,
a small female ghost,
a tortured child in an
immature womanly body.
Feet un-tanned for years
covered by school socks,
fidgeted under the blankets.

On a starless night, next
to a bundle of glands and hormones,
a tiny heart beating wildly
in cold fear,
eyes closed feigning sleep,
parted lips closed by a rough mouth,
the sob swallowed.
Sharp teeth against clenched teeth.
Male hands restraining
fragile childish wrists.
My glass bangles broke,
scratching away ink stains.
Silent lips swelling up
with clotted blood.

When I spoke... finally,
with bleeding lips, I swore.
The voice of the Nun saying,

'The Meek shall inherit the Earth,'
died in the coffin of soft feminine flesh.
Lessons in ink on paper blurred,
lessons on skin were memorized.
My grandfather asked laughingly,
Which bee stung our little flower's lip?

I plucked jasmines
and trampled over them,
my eyes tearless.
I became allergic to
ink pens, milk and dust.
Sleep was unreal,
so were dreams.
I continued to hold classics,
in hands bare without bangles.

Bridal Entry

When I entered your house,
with rings on my toes,
black beaded gold
chain around my neck,
silver bells jingling
on my ankles,
rice grains did not spill,
nor camphor burn.
No eager faces greeting
nor wanting a glimpse,
waited for me.
Nothing, to be exact.

Just a dusty bed
devoid of rose petals awaited me.
Your forearm scarred by my tattooed name
writhed in shame.
I waited in vain
for the black telephone
connected by my umbilical cord,
to sing a lullaby.

Dominic Franks

Dominic Franks graduated from Bangalore Medical College in the monsoon of 2004.

Twenty-six years old, he says, 'I am in love with words. The way they taste in my mouth, on my lips and tongue is better than the choicest foods; but when a man is hungry, finely crafted sentences mean nothing.'

He finds writing more interesting than reading, which according to him is too passive. Poetry had always been the literary genre that he enjoyed the most. Silence, solitude, darkness, experience and people have been his greatest teachers. He loves watching little children at play. The two things he fears the most are losing courage and snoring when he sleeps.

His craze for sports, led him to give up his career in medicine and join ESPN, a premier sports channel, where he works in the Production Department.

How Long

This morning I saw two schoolgirls
in uniforms of red-and-black chequered pinafores
sitting behind their fathers.
One girl's well-oiled hair was done up in pigtails,
the other wore her tresses in double braids.
Long tresses, with a breath of magic, bent double to
craft the perfect loop
which shall bounce vigorously through all the
livelong day.
Sitting astride those scooters, their skirts riding
forever upwards,
I espied the shadow of black down on their legs;
their socks
bunched up at their slender ankles for the elastic was
long since useless,
their legs smooth, contoured and supple –
coloured like the brown of the earth and tinted with
too much sun.

And I wondered… how long?

How long before the absolute conviction in the
goodness of life begins to wither...
How long before the midmorning breeze looses its
humour…
How long before the innocence of childhood is
replaced by the iron trappings of adulthood…
How long before the eyes grow dim and weary…
How long before the smiles the fathers wring turn to
blushes the young boys bring…
How long before they start wanting more than they
have…
How long before they begin to feel 'unfortunate'
and underdone…
How long before they stop being and want to
become -
become something more, become someone else.

And how long before *Remedios jumps off the
leaves which smell of spice and are fragrant with
flowers…
How long before Remedios takes me by the hand
and teaches me once more to be blind.

*Remedios: a character from Gabriel Garcia Marquez's One Hundred
Years of Solitude. A creature of unique beauty, she is utterly unconscious
of the effect her beauty has on people and abides by no social norms - even
with respect to her daily ablutions.

Brave Foot-soldiers of Time

An old lady bent at all joints,
her hair swimming in jasmine flowers,
being helped across the gnarled footpath
by a middle-aged man;
boy scout, son and lover -
all rolled into one.
The twain were heaping
smiles upon each other,
and I gaze hard and peer deep,
my 24 year old eyes brimming
with desolate mirth.

I speak of the satyr in his threadbare suit;
the lady who preens before the mirror
wishing away ugliness;
the school boy running alongside buses
beating out a death lullaby with hope-filled fists
until he is wrenched inside by a
footboard saint amidst the motion of the masses.

I speak of teenage sweethearts
bashful with raging love;
of grandparents renewed with life
at the swelling of wombs;
of office goers treading sad furrows
on buses, trams, subways and footpaths;
of the priest with his incarnadine
chasuble losing faith;
of the pot-bellied poojari cursing the children
who cheat death as he rides to his next pooja;
and of husbands and wives whose marriages
have gone sour....
It is for them I chant my battle anthem.

Then and Now

Heard the train roll by
beside the picket fences,
rumblings sheathed
by eloquent silences.

Hear the traffic treble
my ears are assailed
by the bleating of horns
and automobile wails.

In a thatched hut
upon an earthen floor,
love built homes
upon the green moor.

In a concrete paradise
with gilded balustrades
emotionless fragility –
glass to shards.

When days stretched
and time stood still,
every moment
to the brim was filled.

Now days crash through,
time wings and flies,
but no tender moments
to remember them by.

Saw skirts sashaying about
marble-skinned ankles,
a head of straggly curls
caused no rankles.

See profusion of flesh,
a wet t-shirt dream,
clothes like chains
through flesh they scream.

Heard the sound of a wind
whisper through a harp
and the music of the gods
drifting through the dark.

Hear the clanging of bells
as loudly they toll,
Hear the fraying of nerves,
and the jangling of my soul.

Sat around the fireside
to the telling of the tale
and the warmth of the
family
through the sleet and hail.

Sit through a dinner
and I can't remember
when television conspired
to be a family member.

Cousins and pets,
Hordes of friends,
Every relationship
I was happy to tend.

Now, I sit all alone,
and my time I do pass
conversing with him
in the looking glass.

Summer Song

The drunks adorn the pavement,
percussionist feet tramp by,
highway robbers in business suits
stare bleak with vacant eyes.
The milkman swings himself, his cans
and rattles into the morn.
The earth is blessed with honeydew
and sweet nectar of the gods.
Goddesses sculpted for naked lust,
Gods bearing crowns and spears.
Religion based not on good
but on awe and crippling fear.
'A casanova wind was out last night'
sings the yellow flower-carpeted ground.
'He's still here,' whisper the jacaranda
flowers in a giddy spiral earthbound.
The blue whistle-pipes its trills
into the drumming rain,
its sweetest hymns bring tears of joy
born from the deepest pain.
Rivers of broken-hearted lovers,
the young still have a chance.
But what of satyrs and aging widows
caught in a deathlike trance.
The morning birds hum flute-song
for the leaves tremulous with delight.
Hark! Gnashing of death-ridden souls
and countless un-cried tears of night.
My wandering road is graveyard bound,
so I'll sing, 'farewell, so long.'
As my boot heels echo from your sight,
hear the echo of my summer song.

Google Search

The Delhi winter famous for making grown men
homesick was upon me,
and I had but one thought,
to know what my friends were up to.

So I did a google search....

One had perfected the art of writing poems on
memorial sites for his friends -
he courts friends whom death courts.

One had made a habit of taking to the Consumer
Forum,
companies that promised much and delivered little.

One had invented something, patented it,
floated his own company, to become a young
entrepreneur.

One as a volunteer had visited Nagapattinam, wrote
lilting prose about the sea-folk,
who would not be devastated by devastation.

One had blended the two things that spoke to him
of finesse - silk and coffee,
a strange mix no doubt - wonder how he did that.
One had gone on to become a doctor, cracking
postgraduate entrance exams galore,
surely, just to give others a complex.

One was trying to rekindle a dying art form, telling
stories magnificently,
spinning magical tales to anyone willing to listen.

One confused me no end with her common name,
she sits in swank coffee shops,
smoking menthol cigarettes and reading Dostoevsky.

One eluded my search, but in her place was a fat
woman with same name,
garnering support for the downtrodden, in
crumpled cotton.

And me, where was I?
Too busy googling away my time,
to warrant a mention anywhere.

Sudipta Chatterjee

Sudipta Chatterjee belongs to the West Bengal Civil Service (Executive) Cadre. She is presently working as Assistant Managing Director, West Bengal Tribal Development Corporation. Despite her long working hours, she finds time to paint, write and go on long drives.

An Alumnus of Lady Brabourne College, Calcutta, she experiments with literary and non-literary compositions. Her works have been published in *The Statesman, Woman's Era, Alive, Perfect Living and The Telegraph*. A collection of her poems has been published under the name *Rosewood Fires*.

With her debut novel *Sandcastles*, she was the second-runner up in the e-Author national novel-writing competition launched by Oxford Bookstore, in partnership with Rupa & Co.

Her short stories have been included in the anthology *Curtains*, which features short stories by 9 women writers.

Land of Sand

More rusty gates were crossed
And quiet shops
And laid-back dunes
Of golden sand.
Old Udaipur,
Soul,
Heartland of Rajasthan,
Twisted and turned
Darkly on its narrow lanes.
Its brow dimly lit
With the myths
Of ages,
Muted and wrinkled,
With eager children,
Stale sweat

And half-meals
The place smelled
Of lavender-incense sticks.
Here sells eternal art
In wood, in leather, metal ware.
The rickety state bus rattled on,
Waking up the yellow city
From the torrid slumber
Of its orange afternoon.
The magic of folksongs
Rent the sky
As the priests of snakes, Kalbelias*,
Carrying their portable snake shrines,
Sat back and ate fire
In the opium haze.
The sun turned the colour of sand,
We drank mahua*
Lolling under a heavy jamun* tree
And fought our deep trance,
The sand in our palms
Trickling slowly into memory.

*kalbelias – snake worshipping tribe of Rajasthan
*mahua – intoxicating drink made out of the ochre hued flowers
*jamun – large black berry

Kapil's Garden

One of life's tiny crayons,
He stood under the rainbow
Lost in the lush mango groves of his home
In the curled up fishing village
Bonpukuria, at the back of beyond.
The green mangoes were his own
The light in the leaves, the roots going down
Down into the verdant past
When his father was all alive
And he got to sit on his shoulders
And smell the sun in his hair.
Kapil was fond of gardens,
What with fragments of clouds in his eye
And the flora he nurtured within.
After the boats took away his father
For the last time, into the heart of river Ganga
Kapil resolved to grow a garden in the vacant space
within

A little patch of marigolds,
Tuberoses, sunflowers turning to the sky.
But shades of grey interfered with his colours
In spite of all the weeding and watering,
For the boats kept coming back
Empty.
As Kapil's mother grew pumpkins, ridge-gourds
On their thatched cottage roof,
Kapil attended to the cattle,
His cheeks fragrant
From fruits he plucked for his mother's pickles.
At times, he went around
Vending fresh milk and home-made curd
Vending dreams and carrying his colours
Towards the next watercolour sunrise.
As shades of grey
Kept interfering with him,
Little Kapil tended to his garden.

At the Temple

The mother clung
To the ornamental pillars
Of the holy shrine
And cried.
She warned her unmindful son
To come and pray,
To have the consecrated sweets.
The gods here are very potent,
She informed him
The gods could do anything!
The son,
Living in gasping gusts,
In bits and pieces,
Hadn't made up his mind
About anything,
Not caring for the blurring horizon
Or the creeping darkness about
The trees,
The sun or the moon,
He laughed.
The mother
Blew her conch-shell
Ringing into the distant horizon
And asked the gods
To forgive him.
She lit a diya
And sheltered the flickering flame
Behind her orange pallu
Softly,
Like the lingering twilight.

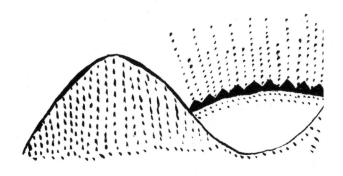

The Hills and Dreaming

These are the snow-capped hills
Of Pemayangste
I had promised you.
There,
Those are the cherry trees
Just like I had said,
And the oranges in bloom.
Wake up from your hangovers
And come outside the guest house walls
I am waiting
With the heavens we still have in common.
There rises the sheer gold of the sun
On the Himalayas,
Putting the Kanchenjungha
And its family of mountain ranges
On fire!
No big deal
If you don't have the morning tea,
Just let me in on your mountain birds!

Up there somewhere,
From the uphill streets
And turns of Gangtok
Along the winding way
To Chhangu lake
Are the dreams
We had hung up on the stars
Like Christmas stockings
Way back!
There beyond the wild flowers,
The orchids,
Are the magic herbs
Of the old man
Of my childhood,
That cure all maladies,
If you don't let the stars of your eyes
Crumble!
We may just as well lose ourselves,
Here,
For ahead
Step by hilly step
Lies our long togetherness.

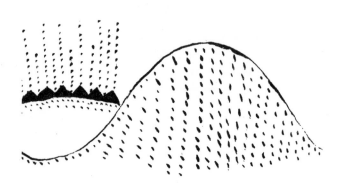

Teesta

Come with your friends
One day
And just reach for the sky
And get your oranges cheap
And cross the Sevak Bridge
Over ethereal, emerald Teesta…
The twisting serpentine vision
Cradled in the heart of the hills,
Then turn a little this way.
Down there
The river gently joins
Its companion Rangit,
Through the gaps in the pines
You can mark the confluence
And find the two rivers
Teesta and Rangit
Frolicking like children
And finding love in endless water.
Pass
Along the tiny momo shops
The assorted liquor bottles
On the greasy glass racks,
Punctured tyres
And the repair garages.
Come and look over the cliff
Downwards,
You can watch me
Fight the frothy surf
On the craggy rocks below
And leave my shells
To fly
Again
Over the sunny hills
And away forever.

Bhuvana Sankaranarayanan

Bhuvana Sankaranarayanan, studied in Sophia High School, Bangalore and then went on to Mount Carmel College. She is a writer, poet and literary critic.

A voracious reader and prolific writer, Bhuvana has written poems for many literary journals and features for Indian dailies including *The Times of India* and *The Deccan Herald*.

As a child she has published poems in the *Children's Digest* and won a prize in a children's competition in the *Illustrated Weekly*. During her journalistic phase she enjoyed exploring the eccentricities of society - its nooks and crevices, and moods of people. As a poet she says, 'I do not just try to observe the world objectively, but delve into the self, deep within, subjectively.'

Kamalamba

My amma's periamma,
Always in nine-yards,
Of hand-woven silken yarn,
With a swatch of sari between her legs,
Wrapped like pants, Iyer style.

I remember looking,
Fascinated by the silken sheen
Of the shimmering parrot green,
As she entered our home
Diamonds and humour sparkling.

She was the soul of utility
On each of my Amma's pregnancies
Bathing the babies
In an hour-long ritual
Feeding Amma fattening ghee.

Graceful in departure too
Packing her bags
To visit the next relative's house
Where they had just heard
The good news.

Watermelon Season

March brings carts
of globules of red and white melons,
moist cushions you can sink your teeth into,
street carts full of desire…
earth shaped, apple-red,
white candy stripes striated,
chilled in glass bowls
heralding the spring collection
of the latest in haute couture
the watermelon colours
being the rage of the season.

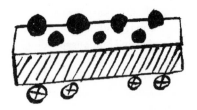

Faith

Immortal mortals, Grecian Hindus,
With flaws and greatness,
Immersed in tragedy, war, comic love or
renunciation.
Mere mortals, earthly men and women
Surrendering to the Will of God,
Praying to the favourite deity,
Rama or Sita,
Blue or pink,
Carved from a single rock,
A phallus or a linga,
Symbols and metaphors
Difficult for the non-believer to interpret,
But believers – illiterate or intellectual
Abjectly address in their hearts,
In moments of dejection or gratitude.
And from the divine, exotic sculpture,
Blooms blessings, the petals of grace…

The Stoic Silence of Sita

Break the stoic silence of Sita,
Oh! Loyal Rukmini,
Complain about your husband,
Open up like a vessel of sealed wax,
Let the Cauvery of torment pour out,
Complain about the Subhadra
In your husband's life,
Mesmerized, listening to her moon-guitar,
Delighting in her cleverness,
While coming home
And beating you black and blue at night…

Wedding Desserts

Cherooti dripping in milk,
Paini, oily paini crumbling in the fingers,
Milk full of floating saffron finger-lets,
Mysore pak
Oozing with ghee,
Saccharine bites
Of Dharwad peda,
Crowned by knowing whispers
Of how many tolas and carats
Bought the IT Techie groom…

Page Three

Pages made of adipose tissue,
The fat tabby cats,
With claw-pens
That make or mar reps,
Jam-spread gossip,
Juicy news,
Succulent bites of life,
Oozing from reality,
Picking the bones of society.

Siamese Kitten

They strayed in through the back door,
Raping the open darkness,
One night when an arrow of Varuna's lightning
Hit the electric pole
And a cassia tree
Pink floss flowers
Tumbled on to our cottage
Breaking the wall
The kittens keened
As rain padded the cell of the garden
Like a jailor with heavy shoes,
Until morning broke
On the damage of the night
And the kittens fled
After gratefully slurping
A saucer of milk…

Subhadra's Mettle

A voice from the Brass-Land,
Singing in a language all can understand,
Desi Tamil platinum metal,
A koel seeking the highest octave to settle.

Strumming the guitar
In a disco of a bar,
Wearing a tight mini,
Her music growing tinny,
This diva stands in Cinnabar circles,
Despairing of the next Live Band bar,
A Damocles' sword.

Srividya

Srividya settled in Coimbatore, is pursuing a doctorate in *'Post colonial literature with special reference to Salman Rushdie.'* She works as a communications trainer, with emphasis on verbal ability. She has been teaching, which according to her is her passion, for the past eight years.

'My poetry recognizes none of the grammar rules I emphasize in my teaching. An unconscious choice but one that I hope makes for a more free interpretation of the words that are not hemmed in by commas or capitals,' she says.

'I can honestly say my life is filled with words. In the form of books, the work I do and the poetry I attempt to create. I say attempt because it is a constant experiment and even 560 odd poems later I can't categorically say I get it. But I get this; my poetry is the most honest part of who I am. And one I am especially proud of.'

the widow

> broken bangles
> hacked off hair
> strewn vermilion
> everywhere
> bereft of persona
> the stench of death
> the soul shivers
> cold and wet
> mocking eyes that see unseen
> the slow eroding
> of reality
> the wails rise
> as the body lifts
> in the maze of memories
> eyes nervously sift
> her child snatched away
> the door tightly shut
> the last vestige of
> the cord is cut
> cast off sent away
> she slowly sighs
> waits for another pain
> waits to die
> waits to die.

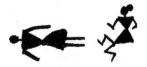

the terrace

the mind works
the heart whispers
hands stilled held by moss-covered bands
soft unyielding
legs clash collide harmonize
find space find their nook
noses align
mouths tremble and are firm
pressed by loving weights
lips part voices hush
breathing jerky but synchronized
heart to heart
like the sea on the sand
everything comes together
the wind howls
the stars shine on a black canvas
below oblivion
the perfect kiss.

seashore

by the ocean far so far away
the sun rises to another bright day
purple glimmers the water far below
and gulls begin to clamour circling the cove
the coconut fronds start swaying
to the beat of the gentle breeze
that embraces all around it
and disturbs the seas
the flowers awaken from their sleep filled night
the birds are getting louder arguing
having a fight
a crab scuttles along the sands on the shore
and from the beach you can hear the ocean roar
pretty pink shells pepper the path i walk on
and the grass feels smooth, a fresh mown lawn
i stand at the cliff's edge
look at the vista before me
the unbearable beauty stretches to eternity
i'd thought I should jump off but
now i step back and stare
and consider myself lucky
lucky that i am there.

vrindavan

on the banks of the river ganga
where man immortality finds
you'll find a house that houses
women of her kind

the shorn hair the rough cloth
are unmistakable traits
proclaim loud and long
the woman's unfortunate fate

she is a w word
not woman, not whore
something more sinister
with a putrefied core

her life has no aim
now that the man is gone
her body is bruised and battered
her soul all tattered and torn

she lives on the banks of the river
watches the waves in the sky
her life quietly seeping
even as the water flows by

in rare moments of togetherness
from solitude her self is freed
shuffled feet and silence
that is her life her creed

from a life of perfect disharmony
the world's at a standstill
her heart cries out for freedom
this solitariness will kill

some of her kind were happy
they have happy memories
they talk with great happiness
till at the guilt they cease

to live and yet not to
to exist therefore to be
a barren piece of ground
in the mesh of reality

so life wasn't a bed of roses before
but at least it was a life
suddenly she just stops being
because she stopped being a wife

in the holy city
she is the eyesore
the pious dip in polluted waters
nothing is sacred anymore

you offer a hand of help
she stares and shakes a no
she is beyond redemption
she is the damned widow.

child's play

        when i was five
        and still alive
        my mother said to me
        you will be married tomorrow
        into that family
                        i don't remember the days
                        there were lots of sweets
                        and harsh words
                        and money i saw my father pay
        the little boy next to me
        ate more sweets than i
        my hair he drenched in red
        there was a shower of rice
                        growing up in my father's yard
                        the heavy cloth slowed my gait
                        the red blaze in my hair
                        portentous to my fate
        a time came when i was sent away
        to live with the man who was my lord
        that is what he is, my mother said
        and snapped the umbilical cord
                        i went alone in a bullock cart
                        hardly a weight on it's yoke
                        going away, all the way
                        i cried emotions evoked
        curious eyes assaulting me
        i cringed and made my way
        everything was normal
        just another mundane day

i was expected
someone smiled at me
showed me a corner
my place it'd be
my new family are farmers
they lived off the land
hardly even touched some feet
a plough was in my hand
under the hot sun in the field
my meeting with the man
my lord funny he seemed
as human as anyone can be
is this the very same boy
who'd eaten more sweets than me
no trace of him remained
him now i could not see
back in the family house
dinner was getting made
after a day's hard work i thought
will i get paid
a dim lamp in the corner
the face in patches of light
it didn't register my whimpers
quieter than the night
there was no lust here
let us not even discuss love
it was a duty he had to fulfill
dictates from above
next day the bruises on my face
told everyone a tale
mother in law was happy
her son was a man to hail

                    the days in the hot sun
                    i was one with the land
                    the nights i clenched my teeth
                    and performed on demand
many a time i'd have thrown up
but held the bile in
this is wrong i'd think
vulgar obscene - a sin
                    from these violent encounters
                    no issue sprung forth
                    a blessing, i thought to myself
                    he'd have only killed us both
one day the man died
drowned in the pond
his mistress went down with him
their entwined bodies were found
                    how old was i can't remember
                    my hair fell around me
                    the four glass bangles cut my arm
                    and blood dripped crazily
then i learnt i was a witch
who'd eaten up her man
i was a girl i'd thought
i didn't understand
                    a bald head and in coarse white
                    i was sent away
                    where was i going i know not
                    they had nothing to say
there is a place where the likes of me
are kept away from society
too cultured to bear the sight
of such form such sobriety

his mistress she drowned with him
a widow's place is born not made
she stood by him no matter what
you destroy the man it's written in your fate
i will die here among my kind
who're all older than me i find
i work the day i work the night
it's a woman this time not man showing might
i wish i had a happy ending for you
but reality isn't fiction what can i do
this is the price of not knowing at all
the living dead wear a white pall

accused

 i was raped today
in an instance innocence swept away
my lover's sweet caress swiftly tossed aside
men just looking for one joy ride
why is this so hard to put down
i was strong i could have sworn
if it was only my body
why is my soul so torn
the laughter and leers so like cheap porn

who was that lady
who said i was to blame
it was my clothes
women like me have a name

a long seated fear horribly brought to light
should i have struggled harder kicked put up a fight
was i at the wrong place at the wrong time
it's all your bad karma sins of your past life
said an old aunt of mine

trapped in the prison of my mind
i watch the man walk free
justice serves everyone
sets rapists at liberty

sudden

i never heard from him again
but then i think of that night
making love being made love to
with no end in sight
i still remember his eyelashes
how they fluttered against my skin
the way he spoke of his lust
his voice salt stirred-in gin
yes i have known pleasure
i am married to my lover you know
but the thrill of new experience
makes for a formidable foe
and so finally i succumbed again
committed adultery like you would say
but regrets i have none
whatever happens come what may
these occasional trysts and rendezvous
add spice to my mundane life
you never know it might be you
seeking a bored wife.

not alone

right now as i am getting bored
    someone's dinner is getting cold
    someone's scared of growing old
    a new sorrow's beginning to unfold
right now as i'm lying in bed
    harsh words are being said
    no one mourns the one who's dead
    someone's going off their head
right now as i'll never get outta here
    someone hides cowering in fear
    hope swiftly unerringly disappears
    no one's around to wipe the tears
right now as i think i feel pain
    someone's being hurt again and again
    there's horror where someone's lain
    someone's methodically driven insane
right now there are others like me
    who have no friends, no family
    not one soul to call their own
    not even god to call on the phone

mumbai monsoon

it happened one mumbai monsoon
i stepped out and into doom
the swirling waters swept me off
with indecent haste
gleeful
maniacal
that impassioned its noxious face
a world unaware to me appeared
made poor all that i feared
the water at least treats each one the same
the merchant the mendicant
the lover the lame
we're all together now
towards the setting sun
heading for the buried bay

Eugene D'Vaz

Born in 1945, Eugene D'Vaz completed his post graduation in English Literature from St Joseph's College, Trichy. He went on to become faculty at the same college where he served the English Department for thirty five years and retired in December, 2003. Post retirement, he realized his life long dream of illustrating and publishing Tagore's *Gitanjali*.

He has been a prolific poet, artist and writer of short stories. Better known as a poet than a painter he says, 'It is easier to publish a poem than exhibit a painting.'

His writings have been published in many leading magazines. He has held exhibitions of his paintings, many of which have been sold abroad, in Trichy, Chennai and Katpadi. He has also done cover designs and logos for various magazines.

The River

Thoughts move breaking across stones
The rains swell them.
Birds hop along the banks
Skim over to catch some indolent fly
Gazing entranced at the illusion of the sky.
The birds come and go
Some linger enchanted by the noise and sparkle
Some speeding across miles
Drop to wet their thirsty bill.

The river moves on
Holding every little memory
Of every little bird
In its course.
There are threatening summers
And endless monsoons
But the way is always there
Filled with the flowing water
Reflecting blue fathomless air.

The Indian Teacher

They listened in rapt silence
As he lectured with tears in his eyes
On hunger and poverty
Humiliation and homeless.
They listened and dreamed
Of how to build a better world.
When the electric bell rang
He gathered his books
Adjusted his tie
Wiped the chalk off his hands
And left the blackboard
Scarred with statistics and graphs.
He turned by the gate
Hungry eyes stared,
The starving child begged
As an old shrivelled man
Sat forlorn, at the foot of a lamppost.

But his class was over.

He went home to his fat lunch
And smiled at the good
Teacher (or preacher) he had become.

Moonloveliness

I wash my hands in the bucket
And think
How things familiar become stale,
Then I look up.
Suddenly caught between the branches
I see the gold disc of the moon.

Tonight's going to be a lovely night.
Closing my eyes, I see
The long winding road
Chequered with the shadows of silent trees
I can even hear
The crunching of my cycle tires on the road
Along which the moon loves to chase me.
Being alone is not good.
Moonloveliness means
You and me on a bicycle
Speeding along moon shadows
Talking of old, familiar scenes.

The Despicable God

He told me
That all he wanted was
To help me with his high contacts.
He would do his best
To see things through –
For nothing, but my good.

He rubbed his palms together
Pulled out a snuff-stained,
Chequered handkerchief
Then loudly blew his nose.
Sizing me up with a shifty look he said,
'Mister, please realize
it's all a matter of your luck.'

As I put my fingers
Deep into my pocket,
The crunch of crisp new notes
Brings forth a hideous smile
Showing vile gaps between yellow teeth.

His smiles have burnt
Deep holes in my pocket.

Sphinx

Silence looms in these corridors
Where you waited once
For someone to draw rainbows.

How frail! How frail and emaciated
These limbs
That toiled and delighted.
Are you waiting for someone
To say goodbye
While you wait on the threshold
Holding the door ajar?

Some other time, may be,
Green paths invited you
And children lisped on your lap.
The children have gone to write
Their own fairy tales.

Why this vain breath to plague the hours?
Those who care
Keep a long vigil
With soaps and creams and cotton,
Watching the skin split in pain
Wound after wound, wound after wound.

If only you had the strength to speak
What would you say?
The clock strikes.
You wait and will not tell –
Only the haunting rhythm of breath
Keeps you tied here.
The ebb goes on
Minute after minute, minute after minute.
Sleep in silence,
Sleep, while we wait.

The Voice of Prophecy

He looked at the congregation
As the morning sun broke
Into blue and green light
Through the glass stained bright.
The altar covered with lace
The book with the gilded edge, lay open.

'My beloved brethren,
I see the skies open
Behold the angels with trumpets
Michael and Gabriel
Followed by fluttering wings –
The Lord of Hosts
Coming in glory
To separate the good from the evil,
The grain from the chaff
The sheep from the goats –
The day of his second coming is at hand.

Yes, my beloved, repent,
If your heart has longed for riches,
Now is the time to ask forgiveness,
For the meek shall inherit the earth.

I see him descend in all glory
On a throne brighter than the shining sun.
Haven't you seen the signs of the times?
Earthquakes, floods,
Famines, plagues,
Wars, murders and bloodshed –
I am calling for your repentance
I am but a voice crying in the wilderness

The prophecies of the Revelation
Shall be fulfilled'.

He wiped his forehead
With a perfumed handkerchief
As they watched him with gaping mouths
Rolling their beads
Mulling over little sins
Begging the Lord for mercy.

'So repent, my children
Let your lives, henceforth be simple,
Sell all that you have
For you shall sit at His right hand
In the Kingdom to come.'

Closing his book he walked out
A barely audible melody
Of latest film hit rang out
From his sleek mobile.

'Hello, good morning,
Yes... oh fine... very good.
Did you bid? That's excellent.
Then it is ours... we have all of it?
Oh good. See you then at the Connemara.'

He opened the door of his new Ford Ikon
Smiling benignly, waving a graceful farewell
Drove away, pursuing thoughts.
The sheep meanwhile, dipped hoofs
In the holy water to absolve their sins
And went bah-bah.

Rain – Memory of you

Outside, beyond the mesh,
Raindrops fall
From the gable of a faraway shed
A crow caws.
I hear the incessant soul-stirring patter of the rain
The tarred road gets darker
The cool gusts set the windmill whirring –
I am reminded
Of that lovely November
When the earth was fair
The wind blew your raven hair
And we held hands.

Time rushes
Down the trickling sands;

That smile never ages;
Fresh with the wildness of youth
I held that hand –
Today raindrops mean
Togetherness,
That faraway scene.

Swetha Prakash

Swetha Prakash is a communication professional based in Bangalore who enjoys writing and painting tremendously.

The winner of the *South Asian Women's Forum Poetry Competition*, her poetry has been published internationally. She specializes in Indian folk art and is proficient in Warli from Maharashtra, Madhubani from Bihar, Saura from Orissa, Pithora from Gujrat, Bengali folk art and Gond from Madhya Pradesh. Swetha has illustrated *Storytelling for Educators* using three folk art styles. She has written and illustrated in Gond, a book for children, *Why Birds Live in the Sky.*

A Dowry Death

When they found her
She was covered with
The redness of her own
Sindoor,
Or was it her bridal
Sari that had so melted,
Unable to withstand
The heat of the stove
Ignited by her
Colourless brother-in-law
Who had hoped, perhaps,
To uncover the
Secret rubies
She held within
Her shy gaze.

Sita's Sorrow

Draupadi, when everyone failed you -
The righteous Yudhistra,
The omnipotent Bhima,
The invincible Arjuna,
And the sweet-natured twins,
You had your faith to lean on,
To shield you
From the violence of those who
Loved you and those
Who didn't.
Whereas I, who was taught
To worship One
and no other,
Was left with nothing -
Not even tears
When he threw me out -
Bag, baggage and babies.

Vignettes

Beggar artist
God painted on rail tracks
Derailed world.

Sewer-scented flower
Rose-colored gutter
Dead girl-woman.

Flowers falling on dry ground
Making way for the future
Duty without attachment.

Spring Monsoon
Dead cattle on torn crops
Lover turned betrayer.

Craft – y

Custom-made,
Rose scented,
Hand-wrapped,
the street vendor claimed
as he sold packets of happiness,
at that busy junction.
My products,
he promised,
are cheaper
than those
pseudo replicas
you get at those
shopping malls,
and to tell the truth
madam, much better.

UNISUN TITLES

Winners: Volume 1 - edited by Mary & Annie Mathew................…......………Rs 125
Brought out in association with the British Council, South India. A prize-winning collection of short stories and poems from the annual *Unisun Creative Writing Competitions* and *The Writers' Circle Prize*.
'The stories in the collection are a good indication of the great potential out there....' *The Literary Review, Hindu*   ISBN 81-88234-11-7

Winners: Volume 2 - edited by Mary & Annie Mathew……...........……..…......Rs 125
Prize winning stories, poems and travelogues brought out in association with the British Council, South India.
Raised voices and sunlit slopes. Blazing eyes and thundering hooves. Desperate strategies in an imaginary war. The celebration of a coastal highway, a requiem for a river... battered bliss, whispering memories. The birth of an artist, the death of childhood. Terror, humour, nostalgia, philosophy...   ISBN 81-88234-25-7

On All Fronts - edited by Gayatri Rao...............…...………….......…...……..Rs 195
Defenders of our nation with stories to tell. Thought provoking, poignant, humorous. If you want to know how weddings are celebrated in Nigeria, or how pigs 'do it.' How wireless equipment can save your life. How to avoid getting seasick on a rolling deck. Why the Air Force insisted on flat shoelaces. An ingenious way of flushing toilets in makeshift army camps. Enjoy this march... voyage... flight... complete with 'armed' escort.
                                    ISBN 81-88234-24-9

The Itinerant Indian - edited by Aruna Nambiar....................…...…….....Rs 295
Hilarious, heart-warming and irreverent. Unusual travelogues: of war protests in Oxford and irate camels in Oman. Balladas in Brasil and burqas on the beach in Bangladesh. Stories of adventure and discovery, of nostalgia and novelty, of mishaps and misery, of confusion and comedy.   ISBN 81-88234-09-5

Curtains: Stories by 9 Women - edited by Gayatri Rao…...…….…......……...Rs 295
An irresistible collection of stories by 9 Indian women. Tranquil backwaters, legends of the hills, the unique world of the Kodavas, the complexity of student life in the US, the Middle-East experience, urban angst and babudom in government offices.
Written with sensitivity and power, they deal with human issues and revel in the sheer pleasure of storytelling.   ISBN 81-88234-10-9

Damini the Damager and other plays by Gautam Raja...............…...………….Rs 125
He's young and restless. His plays are provocative, disturbing and a challenge for actors. With theatre in his blood, greasepaint on his soul, an ear for conversation and an eye for detail, Raja gives us three plays – with memorable characters and metaphors that reverberate...long after the curtain...   ISBN 81-88234-07-9

Heartbeat: 4 Poets - edited by Annie Chandy Mathew.............................Rs 125
Aptly named, this is an endearing little volume introducing four fresh voices in Indian poetry. It features Shaista Yacoob, Arka Mukhopadhyay, Francis Alapatt and Farahdeen Khan. They speak of everyday realities, disillusionment and dreams with an eloquence that will find an echo in your heart.   ISBN 81-88234-12-5

The Peacock's Cry – edited by Karuna Sivasailam...................................Rs 125
This elegant volume features twelve poets from India and outside on a single theme – India and all things that evoke our land and the myriad different ways in which we live, love and die.   ISBN 81-88234-23-0

Looking in, Looking out - by Chandy Mathew......................................Rs 250
A collection of 19 short stories set in different places about different people: young and old, simple and venal, nostalgic and naughty, melancholic and magical. Probing and provocative, never dull.   ISBN 81-88234-04-4

Fireflies in the Dark - by Annie Chandy Mathew.................................Rs 250
A collection of 23 short stories, it sets off the darkness of guilt, exploitation, pain and hatred against the redemptive power of love, hope and the courage to care.
                    ISBN 81-88234-05-2

Sunshine Meals - by Annie Chandy Pallivathuckal.............................Rs 40
This compact introduction to solar cooking is meant for the ordinary individual. It introduces both parabolic cookers and box cookers in easy-to-follow steps. Best of all, it includes a selection of nutritious and mouth-watering recipes from the Indian subcontinent.   ISBN 81-88234-01-X

World Clean Energy: Buyers' Guide and Directory....................................Rs 1300
An authoritative sourcebook to locate providers of clean energy products and services worldwide.   ISBN 81-88234-03-6